Computers All Around Us

Jim Drake

A computer is a machine that can do many things very
quickly. Computers need instructions called programs.
Each program makes a computer do something different.
Computer programs help us to work, have fun, learn new
things and communicate with other people. Computers
are important in many people's lives.

Heinemann
LIBRARY

First published in Great Britain by Heinemann Library,
Halley Court, Jordan Hill, Oxford OX2 8EJ
a division of Reed Educational and Professional
Publishing Ltd.
Heinemann is a registered trademark of Reed Educational
& Professional Publishing Limited.

OXFORD MELBOURNE AUCKLAND
JOHANNESBURG BLANTYRE GABORONE
IBADAN PORTSMOUTH (NH) USA CHICAGO

Designed by Visual Image, Taunton
Printed in Hong Kong

03 02 01 00 99
10 9 8 7 6 5 4 3 2 1

ISBN 0 431 04942 4

British Library Cataloguing in Publication Data

Drake, Jim
    Computers all around us. – (Log on to computers)
    1.Computers – Juvenile literature
    I.Title
    004

    ISBN 0 431 04942 4

Acknowledgements
The Publishers would like to thank the following for
permission to reproduce photographs: BMW (GB) Ltd: p6
(both); British Airways: G Price p11; Trevor Clifford: pp4,
5, 7, 9, 10, 17, 26, 27; Image Bank: p20, N Brown p24, D
Hamilton p25, S Niedorf p8; The Kobal Collection: p29
(both), Disney p28 (right), Paramount Pictures p28 (left);
Pictorial Press Limited: p23; Powerstock: pp12, 19;
Science Photo Library: S Fraser/Main X-ray, Newcastle
General Hospital p15, St Bartholomew's Hospital p14, E
Young p18; Stillview Photography: p22; Tony Stone
Images: E Pritchard p16; Tesco Photographic Unit: p13;
VISA: p21.

Cover illustration by Andy Parker.

Every effort has been made to contact copyright holders of
any material reproduced in this book. Any omissions will
be rectified in subsequent printings if notice is given to the
Publisher.

Any words appearing in the text in bold, **like this**, are
explained in the Glossary.

CONTENTS

WHAT COMPUTERS DO

Computers can help us to work.

A computer is a machine. It cannot do anything without a **program**. Programs are a code that computers can understand. Different programs can make the same computer do different things. This book is about some of the ways computers can help us.

Computers can store lots of information then change it or send it to someone else very quickly. The words in this book were typed using a **word processor** program. When the writer finished work, he played on a games program. Computers never get tired and don't need to sleep.

Computers can help us to play.

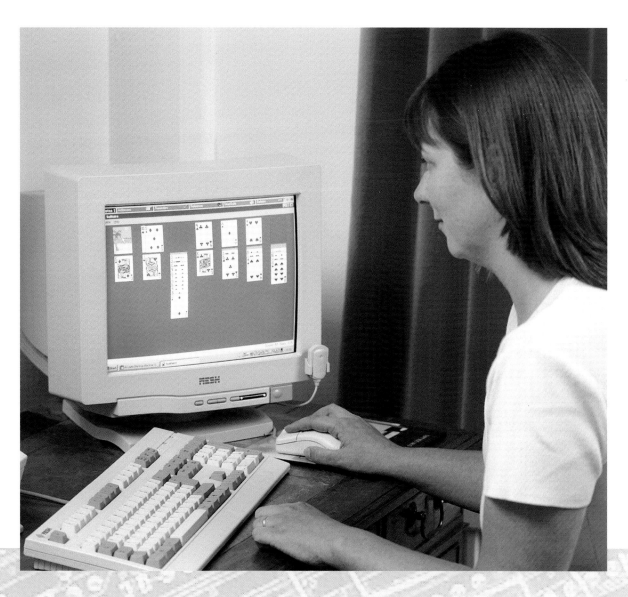

HIDDEN COMPUTERS

Lots of the machines we use have **microprocessors** hidden inside them. A microprocessor is like a tiny computer. Modern cars often have a microprocessor to keep the engine working properly. This can help to save petrol. It can tell a mechanic if something needs repairing.

Microprocessors can make car engines and brakes work better.

Many of the things we use in our homes are controlled by microprocessors. In a washing machine, a microprocessor can let the right amount of water in. It can check to make sure the water is not too hot or cold. Different **programs** are needed for different clothes.

This microprocessor controls a video recorder.

COMPUTERS IN THE HOME

Many people have a computer at home. Some people do all their work from home, using a computer. People can send work to you and you can send messages to other people using **E-mail**. **Video conferencing** lets you see and talk to people all over the world.

These people can talk as if they were in the same room. They could be in different countries.

Many home computers are used for playing games. A computer game is just a **program**. A games console, like a Playstation™, Nintendo™ or Sega™, is a computer made specially for playing games. They don't have keyboards but they use gamepads which can be held in your hand.

This is another kind of computer. It is used for playing games.

COMPUTERS IN THE OFFICE

Computers have made work easier for many people in offices. Most office work needs to be saved. Information can be stored on computer **disks** or **CD-ROMs** instead of paper. One CD-ROM can store as much information as a whole shelf of books. This means that trees don't get chopped down to make the paper.

This disk drive can store as much information as hundreds of these filing cabinets.

Computers in an office can be joined in a **network** so everyone can share the information. Many people can work on a project at the same time. In some offices, people don't have their own desks. They can '**log in**' to any computer.

In this office your work comes to you, wherever you sit.

COMPUTERS IN SHOPS

A computer works out our shopping bills.

Nearly all shops use computers. Small shops often have a **microprocessor** in the till. This counts how much money the till has in it. In bigger shops, like supermarkets, more of the work is done by computers.

Imagine you buy a bar of chocolate in a supermarket. A **bar-code** reader tells a computer what has been bought. The computer looks up the price and adds it to the bill. The computer can even work out when it is time for the shop to order more chocolate.

Scanning stock in a supermarket. Later, the bar-code reader will be connected to a computer which will work out how much stock there is.

COMPUTERS IN MEDICINE

Computers can help doctors and nurses in many ways. Your doctor probably keeps notes about you on a computer. A computer can remember when people need special tests. It can even send a letter to tell them. Doctors and patients can use the **Internet** to find out about diseases and new medicines.

A nurse can check to see which medicines you should or shouldn't have.

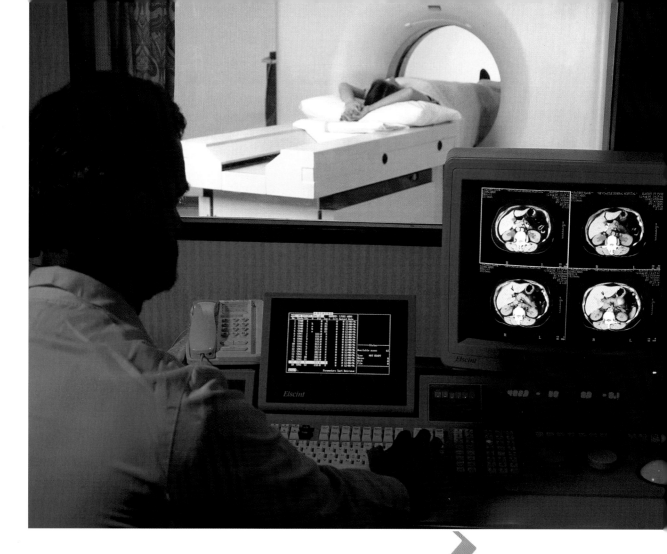

Some special medical equipment needs computers to make it work. A CAT scan uses X-rays. A computer makes the scan into pictures to give doctors a clear view inside the body. **Virtual reality** can help doctors to learn new operations. They can try it out on a computer screen. It's a bit like a computer game!

A CAT scan shows the doctor what's inside the patient's body.

COMPUTERS IN TRANSPORT

Computers help us move around. Some traffic lights are controlled by a computer. They can work out which traffic to let through and can change traffic lights, especially for ambulances or fire engines. Computers show air traffic controllers where planes are. They can give a warning if they get too close to each other.

If there is a traffic jam, a computer can change the lights to let more cars through.

In a travel agency you will see lots of computer screens. A computer can check to see if any plane seats are free. It can then print a ticket for you. This makes sure that every passenger has a seat. With a home computer connected to the **Internet** you can book your own plane seats from home.

A travel agent can see if there are empty seats on a plane.

COMPUTERS IN FACTORIES

Many computers are used in factories. Some are in the factory offices. They work out how much to pay the workers. They can store the records that the factory needs, like orders from customers. Factories also use computers to help design new products.

Computers can draw new designs very quickly. The computer can show a very detailed picture of the new design.

Some factories use robots. A robot is a machine that doesn't need a person to control it. A computer tells the robot what to do. If you change the **program** in the computer, the robot will do a different job. Robots are good for dirty and dangerous jobs like paint spraying and working with metal.

Some people worry about losing their jobs because robots can do their work and don't need to sleep or eat.

COMPUTERS AND MONEY

You can get money from ATMs all over the world. If someone else discovers your **PIN** number and steals your bank card, they can use them to take your money from the bank.

Computers are very quick at adding up. Banks use computers to keep track of people's money. An ATM (Automated Teller Machine) can give you money. You put in your card and enter a secret '**PIN**' number. The bank's computer checks the number and that you have enough money in your account.

Credit and debit cards let us buy things without money. A computer moves money from your bank account straight to the shop's bank account. 'Smart cards' have a **microprocessor** inside the card. You fill the card up with money from your bank account. The microprocessor works out how much money is left each day.

Credit cards mean that people can buy things without having to carry lots of money around.

COMPUTERS AND DISABILITY

Computers can help disabled people. A **GPS** system acts like a map for blind people. You tell the computer where you want to go. Satellites above the Earth tell the computer exactly where you are. The computer stores a map and can work out where you should be. If you go the wrong way, the computer will warn you.

This blind person is using a GPS. He can find his way without anyone else's help.

This man has a disease that stops his muscles working. He uses a computer voice to speak.

Computers can turn writing into speech. People who have trouble speaking write on a keyboard and the computer speaks for them. Computer voices don't sound like real people yet. Computers can help people to control their wheelchairs if they can't use their arms and legs. They can even work artificial legs.

THE INTERNET

The **Internet** is a way of joining computers all over the world. A computer connected to the Internet can send messages, called **E-mail**, to another computer. People can send E-mail messages all over the world. E-mail can have pictures and sounds as well as words.

E-mail can travel anywhere in the world at any time of day. You don't need to wait for a postal delivery.

The World-wide Web is part of the Internet. **Web sites** contain information about all sorts of things. You need a special **program** called a browser to read web pages. There are millions of different web sites so it can be hard to find the one you want.

PROBLEMS WITH COMPUTERS

Computers sometimes go wrong. A mistake in a **program** is called a bug. This can make the whole computer **crash**. You may have to turn the computer off and start it up again. A virus is a nasty program that can make a computer crash. It is a bit like a disease that computers can catch. Viruses can be passed from one computer to another on **disks**.

This computer has crashed. Sometimes you lose all the work you have done.

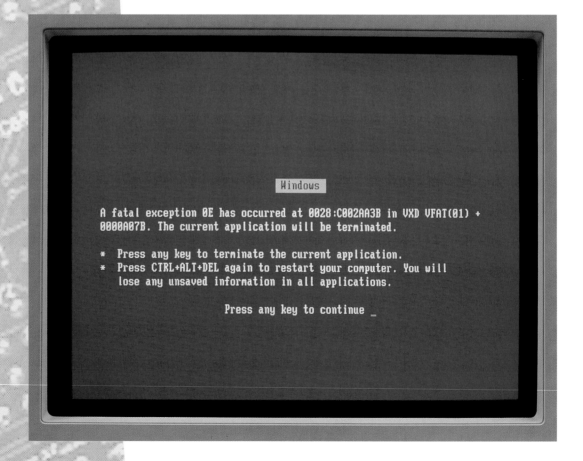

```
                    Windows

A fatal exception 0E has occurred at 0028:C002AA3B in VXD VFAT(01) +
0000A07B. The current application will be terminated.

*   Press any key to terminate the current application.
*   Press CTRL+ALT+DEL again to restart your computer. You will
    lose any unsaved information in all applications.

                Press any key to continue _
```

Some computers can only understand dates up to 1999. This is sometimes called the Millennium Bug. If the computer is meant to send people letters or bills on a certain day in the year 2000, they won't get sent.

A virus can destroy all the information stored on computer. Anti-virus programs are like medicine for 'sick' computers.

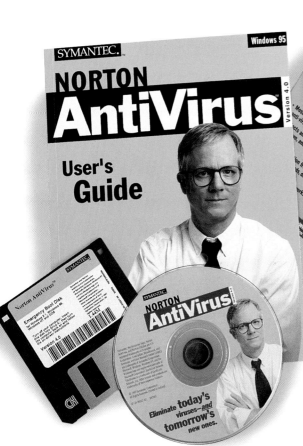

WHAT NEXT?

New computers get more powerful every year. No-one really knows what they will be able to do when you are grown up. We can guess that computers will be able to do much more. Writers and film-makers try to imagine what will happen but nobody ever gets it all right!

No-one knows what the future will bring. We can only guess.

Some people believe that everyone will stay indoors and do everything by computer. We might have robot servants to do all the work. Money and shops could go out of date. We could buy everything through the **Internet** and pay by credit card.

GLOSSARY

bar-code   a pattern of dark lines that stands for a number. A bar-code reader can turn it into computer code.

CD-ROM   shiny disc that can store words, pictures and music

crash   when a program goes wrong and the computer stops working

disk   disks store information and programs when a computer is turned off

E-mail   short for electronic mail messages (words, pictures and sound) sent between computers

Internet   a huge network that links computers all over the world

log in   joining to a network. You usually need to give your name and a password.

microprocessor the brains of a computer. It does whatever a program tells it.

network a way of joining computers so that they can send messages to each other along wires. Computers on a network can share programs.

PIN short for Personal Identification Number, a secret number that you need to use a bank card

program the instructions that tell a computer what to do

video conferencing connecting people so that they can see and hear each other on their computer screens

virtual reality using computers to create illusions, so you can see things that are not really there

web sites special programs on computers connected to the World-wide Web. Each web site has its own address and contains information.

word processor a kind of program that helps us to write

INDEX